T0078025

THE KID WHO HAD LIFE STACKED AGAINST HIM

CRYING TO THE TOP

DERRICK REYNOLDS

authorHOUSE

AuthorHouse™
1663 Liberty Drive
Bloomington, IN 47403
www.authorhouse.com
Phone: 833-262-8899

Published by AuthorHouse 10/25/2021

ISBN: 978-1-6655-4248-7 (sc)
ISBN: 978-1-6655-4300-2 (hc)
ISBN: 978-1-6655-4249-4 (e)

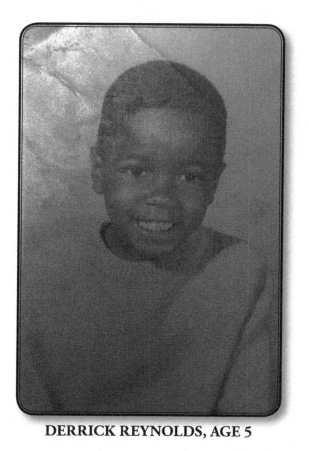

DERRICK REYNOLDS, AGE 5

CONTENTS

DEDICATION

I want to dedicate this book to my grandpa, Ollie James Reynolds, and my grandma, Doris Helen Reynolds.

INTRODUCTION

Life is harder for some of us than others. This is the true story about a boy who started out life without much more than his salesmanship and his grandpa teaching him about how to be a man.

Over the years, Derrick Reynolds grew into a man who found himself the single father of his two boys.

Read his story to find out how he went from a rough start as a kid being raised by his grandparents, through a failed marriage, to being happily married to the love of his life, Lee Nora, and became a highly successful salesman and businessman while raising their four boys together.

Also, if you need a coach, or someone who can help motivate you or your team, please reach out via the email address listed below.

And, if you have a business and you need help increasing your profits, you can email DrSuccess509@gmail.com for guidance and services today.

CHAPTER 1

A ROUGH START

CHAPTER 1

When I was four years old, I attended Lowell Preschool, and I would act like I was sick so I could go home early. It worked the first time, so I thought I would try it again. After that first time, it became easy.

I went home so often that the school decided I needed to be seen by a physician. As it turned out, I had asthma. I guess that's what I get for playing sick and trying to go home, because I was so shy and scared that I didn't want to go to school.

In my elementary years, I was just trying to figure things out. I always wondered why I didn't ever have any money, and my friends always had money, and so did their moms and dads—but that always bothered me.

My journey is about not giving up. In the following pages, you'll read about how I went from being thrown out of my home in the middle of the night to where I am today, making six figures a year. And that's not the end, so keep reading! That's what this book is about, and I hope it will inspire you to keep going, don't give up, and don't quit.

When my sister and I were around 2nd and 3rd grade, my stepdad and my mom got into it at a club. My stepfather walked all the way home from the club that night and put my sister and me out of the house. We were just seven and eight years old, and he did it because we weren't "his" kids.

We were not his biological kids. Of course, he didn't put out his own three kids. You know, that's bullshit, what he did. It really got inside my head—how could any sane human do that to a child? We could have been kidnapped or killed. That just wasn't right what he did to us. My sister and I ran so fast to our grandparents' house—and it was about a half-mile—one block is just too long for someone to put out two young kids at 4 o'clock in the morning.

This was just one of the challenges that I had to get through from my past, and I finally did. The night my stepdad put my sister and me out of the house late at night, I remember waking up thinking I was dreaming. When I realized I wasn't dreaming and this was really happening, time just stopped. I looked into my stepdad's eyes—this short man looked like the devil himself. He told my sister and me we needed to get the hell out of his house. We opened the door. It seemed like we stepped into another world. It was so dark, and no air was blowing, I couldn't hear anything— no crickets, or birds chirping, or anything moving.

My driveway had a dip at the bottom. It seemed like we were moving in slow motion as we had to run up this big hill. We didn't have to cross any busy street. We never knew where our mother was, but we knew we had to run fast. I think I wet myself because I was so, so scared. We were in survival mode. We ran so fast, I guarantee you we could have beat any Olympian that night. I remember seeing the stoplight change. I only saw it for a half-second because we were running so fast.

We finally arrived at my grandparents' house. That weekend we had family visiting from Wichita, KS, one of which was my grandfather's brother. My grandfather had a fit when he found out we were put out of the house at that time of the night. My grandfather grabbed his gun, but his brother wouldn't let him go. I felt like I was escaping from jail, and I never want to feel like that again.

My sister died in December 2019. She was 11 months older than me. We were Siamese twins. I wish I could tell my sister that she didn't do anything wrong. It was that crazy stepdad from Louisiana; I'm sure he was possessed.

I felt my grandfather was hard on me.

So, I was raised by my grandparents. My grandfather dropped out of high school in the 9th grade to help take care of his brothers and sisters. He met my grandmother when she was in the 8th grade. Shortly after that, she became pregnant with my mother, then she dropped out of school. So they were going to struggle as a young family. They really struggled because they were just kids themselves.

Eventually, I figured out why my grandfather was so hard on me. But, at the time, I didn't really understand it. In the summer, when school was out, other kids would be heading to the swimming pools—not Derrick. No, Grandpa had me working the summer program designed for low-income families to earn money and learn new skills to keep them out of trouble.

I felt slighted and like I was being done wrong.

I remember one day before I got off work, I made a decision—that day, they taught us how to buff floors—I worked at an elementary school. When I got off work, I told my grandfather I was going to quit that job because they had us buffing floors all day, and my grandfather said, "You aren't going to quit, but you will be the first one at work tomorrow." The next morning he loaded up my bicycle in his truck and drove me to work.

Guess what? I was the first one there that day. I had to wait outside until someone arrived to open up the building. Although I was small and didn't want to work, my manager was a big muscular guy who liked to work kids to death. I didn't quit; I actually learned something new, and one day I might have to use that skill to make a living. Always be learning! You can never learn too much.

My grandfather was teaching me to be a man because he had to grow up so early, taking care of a family at 16, and he knew that he wouldn't be here forever to take care of me.

During this part of my life, I was looking for something I didn't know existed, so I joined the football team. I was wanting to punish someone on the football field, because I was thirsty for success.

CHAPTER 2

SALESMANSHIP

CHAPTER 2

This is when the salesmanship started to come out.

I remember playing this one football game against the Whitney Bears; I was playing the center position. It's not the position I wanted to play. My coach kept calling pass plays, and none of the receivers could catch the ball. I asked the coach if I could try to catch the football. The coach basically said, "What the hell, he can't be any worse than the other receivers. They aren't catching anything anyway." So he gave me a chance at it.

I moved into position as receiver to catch the football. The first time they called a play to me, I was saying to myself, "No pressure," because I knew if I dropped the football, I would be moved back to the center position. So, they threw the football to me. I caught the football, and when I scored a 75-yard touchdown, my football career changed forever.

They threw another pass to me, and I scored again. It was a wrap—I took the position forever. It built my character and my confidence to be able to show myself I can do anything if I set my mind to it. I learned early if you want something, you have to go get it.

It was really hot out there on the football field, and I knew everyone else was tired, so I knew I had to outwork them. I made the decision to ask for what I wanted, and I had wanted that new position, so I asked for an opportunity like I have had to do all my life, and I got it.

In junior high, I was tired of being poor and eating in the free lunch line.

This was the beginning of me selling me.

So, when I was in the 7th grade, I started to sell gum at school to have money to eat and get some extra cookies or a bowl of french fries. I would buy a pack of gum for 25 cents. Then I would sell the gum for $1.00. Boy, was I rich and rolling! I started buying four packs of gum when Bubblicious was popular. Grape was the top seller, then strawberry.

These kids at Thomas Edison High School had money. Their parents were doctors, lawyers, and engineers—but then there was me, being raised by grandparents that only made it to the 8th and 9th grades. What I liked about those rich kids was they never had any change, so instead of buying one piece for 25 cents, they would give me $1.00. So, then I was making $5.00 a pack versus $1.00. Remember, these kids could go to the store themselves and get a pack of gum for 25 cents a pack!

My profits were 500 percent, so I raised my prices to $1.00 apiece. I wanted to make money honestly, so I tried an idea, and it stuck. I couldn't wait to go to school every day now so I could make money. And, I really slept well at night knowing I made some money for my efforts and did not ever beg anyone for money. Making a little money made me want to go to college and get a degree to make big money.

I got a job my junior year in high school so I could pay my car insurance. My grandfather bought me a '74 Maverick. I was so proud of it, and I took good care of it. My grandfather said, "Don't move that car until you get a job and pay the car insurance and buy your gas."

I just thought that was what parents do, but I see today what my grandfather was trying to do was make a man out of me. When my grandfather bought my first car, I thought I was *the* man. I wish I could thank him again because that car taught me many responsibilities at an early age. Some of my friends were busy taking care of babies early. I was taking care of *my baby*—my '74 Maverick car.

My high school was about 20 miles from my north Tulsa home. One day in 9th grade, we finished practice late, and it was dark. My friend's mom came to pick him up. We were at the back of the school. My friend said I could catch a ride with him. But, when everyone got in, it was a really tight fit. His mother asked him whose all moms had given him a ride before. My mom was the only mom who hadn't given anyone a ride. His mother told me to get out of her car.

It was pitch-black dark behind the school, so I started to cry. What a damn-awful thing to say to a kid! I guess she felt bad and told me to get back in the car. I mean, who puts a kid out in the dark? I was a young man with high expectations to be knocked down by this woman who told me to get out of the car and was going to leave me behind a dark high school building. I felt like I wanted to die at that moment, and if she left me, I probably would have been killed by someone, so God was looking over me.

The next day in school, I wanted to quit sports, but I had a sweet godmother named Gwen Lewis who talked me out of it. She watched out for me during football and basketball season, and another couple, Mr. and Mrs. Brown, took my mother's turn during basketball season.

In my senior year, I wasn't sure what I wanted to do with my life. My grades were average, mostly C's and some A's, and B's also, so I went to the guidance counselor to talk about college. The lady said, "With your grades, you won't be able to survive college."

I WOULDN'T DISCOURAGE ANY KID LIKE THAT. FORTUNATELY, IT WASN'T ENOUGH TO STOP ME.

I went to talk to my grandfather then, who told me that I wasn't college material, and I needed to go into the Army. I was so dejected by this because my grandfather was my world. So, I went and talked to my cousin Greg because he was in the Army. He told me *not* to go into the Army because the Army is not a place for a black man. My cousin said that the only reason he went to the Army was because he wasn't doing anything with himself, and after high school, he started getting into trouble. My cousin said he would kick my BUTT if I went into the Army. So, I thought about it a lot but decided not to go into the Army, even though that's what my grandfather had told me to do.

While working at McDonald's between my junior and senior years, I was doing good playing football and maintaining my grades. And, at the time, I went to Thomas Edison High School in Tulsa, OK, which was really a good school.

Then, about that time, my grandfather got sick. He found out he had cancer my senior year, just as I was about to graduate high school. My grandfather's health was failing fast. After he would get off work, he'd head home. Then he would pull into the yard and be so sick he couldn't get out of his truck to walk into the house. He had to sit in the truck for about thirty minutes because he was in so much pain from the cancer. I would go out there to him and say, "Grandpa, are you okay? I will help you, Grandpa."

And he would say, "That's okay, son, let me sit here. I will gain my strength in a little while."

I knew things were going to get worse. Then I started to realize, **"*This* is why my grandfather was so hard on me, for these moments, to help me become a man because I was about to be on my own."**

Around this time, my grandfather said to me, "I'm leaving my two trucks for you to sell, so you and your grandma will have some money until she can get a check started." It was then I knew it was close to the end.

CHAPTER 3

STAMINA

CHAPTER 3

—◆—

This starts my stamina.

Around that time, I remember another thing that happened to me that was traumatic. I came home from school one day, and my grandmother was holding the mail when I walked in the door. My grandmother said, "You're in trouble, and you're going to be in more trouble when your grandfather gets home from work."

I knew he got off work at 6:00 and would get home about 6:30 p.m. every night. So I said to my grandmother, "What did I do?"

"This letter. You went over to McClain High School and assaulted an officer?"

I was a quiet kid, and that school had some rough kids there that would hurt you in a minute.

My grandfather came home, and my grandmother gave him that letter. He read it, and it said I had to appear in court. His words to me were, verbatim, "I believe you, son. I know you didn't do it." I was already in tears and pleading my case to him. But he said, "If you did it, I know you would never do anything like that again." And I knew if I did anything like that, I would get a butt whooping.

So, I went to court the next week. The person that actually did it used my name, and their height and weight were the same as mine. I had always missed a lot of school because I was sick from asthma, which I found out I had when I was five years old during the time I was faking being sick.

The only thing that saved me was that I was actually in school that day. The probation counselor called my high school and checked to see if I was in school that day, and I was. I was accused of assaulting a school officer—that's a serious charge. My high school confirmed I was there in

English class during the time. This happened at 11:00 a.m., so the charges were dropped. I was so freaking mad about that whole situation! I have never been in trouble in my life. But, the ordeal made me stronger.

Pleading my case to prove myself and getting ready for life.

Remember, when I went to my high school guidance counselor to check on colleges, she told me I wouldn't be able to handle college because of my grades and poor scores.

When I went to Northeastern State University to enroll, I had to talk to their school counselors to talk about why they should let me into their school.

I told them I wanted to do better in life, and I let them know my neighborhood had gangs everywhere.

I told them how I was raised by my grandparents and that my grandfather had a 9th-grade education, and my grandmother had an 8th-grade education. I let them know that he had to go to work early, and shortly after that, my grandmother became pregnant with my mother in the 9th grade, so she quit school to take care of her baby.

I also let them know I didn't want football to be the only thing I could do to be successful. I told them in the African American family, they say we made it if you make it to the 12th grade and graduate and don't go to jail. Then, I told the panel I wanted to better myself if they would give me the chance. So, they said they would give me a chance, and I was so excited! But, the university let me in on academic probation, so I had to keep my grades up.

You may have noticed I haven't mentioned my mother since the story about the night my stepdad threw my sister and me out into the street when we were just seven and eight years old. Our mother had five kids by age 28. I had enrolled myself in college. My Mom did a wonderful job with her 5 kids, she has always been proud of her kids.

During college, I was always really hungry. We had meal points, but they had to last me all semester because I didn't have any extra money. I never ate breakfast during the entire semester. For lunch, I would get two

Coney dogs—one with shredded cheese and one with melted cheese—with a bag of chips and a mountain dew pop. My dinner was also pretty slim.

During the two years I was there, no one sent any money because my grandfather had died, and it was survival, baby. I had nobody.

However, I remember this one time my aunt told me she had sent me two dollars in the mail. She said, "When you get the money, go to Sonic and buy yourself a big footlong hot dog." And when the two dollars came in, I thought I was in heaven. I went to Sonic and enjoyed my footlong hot dog.

I really want you to think about that for a minute. Two dollars. In two full years of college, that averages one dollar a year for spending money—that's my story!!

My uncle was my role model then. When I came home on the weekends, I would go over to his house to wash my clothes. It was nice, but then my uncle got on drugs and went off the deep end. So now, I had lost my uncle, and my grandpa had died on the day I graduated high school.

The next day after he died, I felt life change for me. I remember one day before my grandfather died, I had said to him, "I got all the girls."

He told me, "Son, those girls aren't putting any money in your pockets." So I learned right then I had to make my own money.

I didn't work while I was in college. I played football but wasn't getting any playing time. I probably should have gotten a job, but football was what was giving me my drive. I had to keep up my grades. I remember after my first semester of college, I had to meet with the school counselors again. They were puzzled by my grades because I had four A's and two F's. I had entered college on academic probation, so because of my grades, they kept me on probation.

After that semester, I picked up the pace on my grades, and with hard work, I finally got off academic probation. My second year, while working for the summer at home, I had a kid on the way, and things started looking downward again. This was the start of my life.

I'm selling again! I'm selling myself.

The judge asked me, "If I were to grant your kids to you, how would you support them?"

I told the judge that it was time for my kids and me to move on, so he granted me temporary custody.

I was working at an Oil & Gas company named Samson Resources, making no money. I started working in the records department. I was making $6.35 an hour. I will never forget that. Back in the 80s, the raises were small, and after a couple of years, I was making $6.55 an hour.

I wouldn't ever discourage any kid. I want to say to everyone: **Don't let anyone discourage you if you have a goal in mind**. Go for it, and don't stop until you get there. For example, my aunt told me to stay at the Oil & Gas Company because I had a guaranteed paycheck every two weeks versus me leaving for a commission sales job. I was making more money on my part-time sales job. So, I left the guaranteed Oil & Gas job to go sell appliances at Brand Central.

I say from me to you: **Take risks or chances sometimes—you can find what you're good at.**

Here I go selling again.

So, I would look at the job board and apply for a job, and they would say, "Derrick, we would give you the job; you're a good worker, but you don't have a degree."

The 5th time I applied for an accounting job, they said, "We just can't turn you down; you're a good guy and a hard worker." Granted, that was during the time I was going through difficult times. The only stipulation was that I had to complete 9 hours of accounting classes because I didn't have any accounting experience. So, I enrolled in the community college and took an accounting class.

At the end of the first day, the teacher said, "Take a sheet of paper out; we're going to have a quiz." That was my first and last day, because I dropped that class. It was too advanced, and my mind just wasn't right.

I had met a young lady who was 21, and I was 26. This was when I had met the true love of my life, Lee Nora Fields.

We worked together at Samson Resources, the Oil & Gas Company I mentioned that I worked at. We weren't dating just yet, and I was always broke because I was paying child support.

She would come by my desk and ask if I wanted to go to lunch, and I would always say, "No," because I didn't have any money. Then after we started dating, she would still come by and ask if I wanted to go to lunch with her. After coming by a couple of times asking about going to lunch and me saying no, I would be so hungry I couldn't afford to pay attention.

So she again came by, and this time she said, "What do you like to eat?"

And I said, "Coney I-Lander," which are these great hot dogs, so she brought back four of them to my desk. When she did, I said, "Thank you, I will pay you back."

"That's okay," she said. I think that was her way of flirting. When she handed me those four Coney's, I was trying to be nonchalant, but then she said, "Bye, I'll see you later." Before she even got to the door, I had swallowed two of those Coney's because I was so hungry, and I don't remember even chewing them.

I took her through some things. We got married, and she got pregnant pretty quickly. She was also raising my two kids after I gained full custody of my boys.

Lee Nora was taking 19 credit hours of college. So now, it was her last semester, and she was helping me raise my kids and was also pregnant with our 3rd child.

She graduated college with a Bachelor of Science in Business Administration in December 1995, and we're still together after 26 years.

CHAPTER 4

DETERMINED NOT TO QUIT

CHAPTER 4

———∿———

Being determined not to quit.

B ack before we were married Lee Nora said to me, "I know you were a jock and didn't get good grades."

I told her, "I had good grades."

So she said, "We're going to Northeastern University to check on your grades. If your grades are good, you're going back to college."

I was mad then, and I told her my mom is at home and I wouldn't have any support, not knowing this is the best thing that could have ever happened to me.

Lee Nora thought my grades were bad.

Things started looking up until her mom and dad turned against her. Lee Nora moved to Tulsa from a little town called Checotah, OK, about 80 miles from Tulsa, OK. You may have heard of Checotah; it's known for Carrie Underwood because she used to live there.

Anyway, Lee Nora's parent's wanted a better partner. I can understand today, but back then, I just couldn't understand it because she was happy. As I said before, I was 26, and she was 21 and about to graduate college. They took her car (that she was paying for) from her. I had a truck which was an old bucket, and I had an old crappy house someone was letting me rent. The child support I had to pay at the time was killing me financially. So, I started cutting yards to afford to buy some groceries and get some gas. Working two jobs was killing me, too.

I felt things were going pretty well between Lee Nora and me, so we moved in together—then all hell broke loose. Her parents disowned her because of a man trying to do the right thing and be a productive citizen of the United States. Many people, and life itself, can really break you down.

I remember one Saturday I was working overtime, but I had to leave at noon because I had to get some tires for my truck from K-Mart. I was sitting in the waiting room, and I spoke to this older lady who was already there. I told her I wished I could have stayed at work. Then she said, "Oh, you have a job?"

"Yes, ma'am."

"I thought all blacks didn't work? Every time I turn on the news, all I see is blacks on there." This was a time to educate her.

I said, "All black men aren't bad; there are a lot of successful black men, you just don't hear about them." Then I told her I couldn't go home and see my kids because I was sitting there.

Then she started again, "Oh, you have a house?"

I wanted to say, "I guess I must have just come up from under a rock," but I was nice, so I was able to educate the lady. That day, I was able to see how some people really feel about black men.

Lee Nora graduated and kept pushing me to be the person I was trying to be.

I remember being so frustrated as I was going into my Economics class one day, I asked my teacher if I could talk to him and told him I wanted to quit. He said, "Son, you can quit, but remember: a person with a degree is always going to get a look before someone without a degree and make more money."

Then I told him, "Thank you," and I sat down in the front row of the class. If he had said, "Go ahead and quit, it will be alright," I probably would have quit. Again, I was truly happy to have someone in my corner.

So, after I went back to school, I only needed 12 credit hours to get my Associate's Degree. I completed it, so then I had an Associate's Degree. I felt unstoppable, and I owed it all to Lee Nora. As my girlfriend at the time, she saw something in me and pushed me to go back and become better.

After that, I enrolled in Langston University once I had my Associate's degree, and I was becoming a "man" by working all day and going to school at night. I liked what I was becoming.

In one of my business classes, we debated whether it was better to have a degree or not, to make more money. So I said, "You don't have to have a degree to make a lot of money." And, at the time, I didn't have my degree yet.

Then the instructor asked, "What if the student that's making a lot of money loses their job?"

The class was like, "That ain't going to happen."

Guess what? I was *that* student making a lot of money working for a large retailer selling appliances, and I got fired because of jealousy. I was making more money than the store manager, and they fired me because I price matched Circuit City. I had a customer go there and come back saying they wanted free delivery, and I told them I couldn't do that, but I offered to price match her dryer cord because dryers don't come with cords.

Later that afternoon, Loss Prevention had me come in and sit down to fill out a report against that customer who had just left. They were trying to find a way to fire me. So, I filled out the report honestly, and they took it. I told them I had been sitting there too long, and I was losing business on the floor because we had a good sale going on at the time. After about thirty minutes, five people came into the room with me, and a couple of them were my friends. I remember their words, "I'm sorry," as this paper was laid out, which I could see before they put it on the desk had big black letters printed across it saying, "termination."

Because I gave the customer that dryer cord as a price match, they were letting me go. I said to them, "You're firing me over $19.99? Here's $20.00 out of my pocket. I have never been in trouble; don't I even get a warning or a slap on the hand?"

And they said no because if it had been inventory time, they wouldn't have been able to find it, which I know was bologna. I was the Michael Jordan of the appliance department. I went to Chicago and made company videos as one of the top salesmen in the nation.

After they fired me, the next day, I went to pick up my final check, which wasn't ready that Sunday. They said it wouldn't be ready until Friday.

The store manager said if he had been there, he could have saved my job. If that was the case, he could have saved it the next day, so I'm sure that was B.S. He couldn't stand that a salesman was making more money than him. He had said it to me before. I'm sure my problems started because I used to drive my old truck to work, and the day before this happened, I bought a brand new Jeep Cherokee (that's when they first came out) and drove it to work. I was fired the next day.

If you buy something, and people around you are jealous because you're trying to do better, just drive your old car or truck and leave the new one at home. And know that you have several friends who are supportive of you.

⸺•◦◦•⸺

While I was going to Langston University, things were getting tight, and I had lost my job, so I had to start over. I was eating at Carl's Jr., which is a hamburger place. I had gone to work at Circuit City appliances then, and it paid the bills, but that was it. I didn't like that place.

While eating, I saw a guy I knew from high school. We went to different high schools, but I knew him. I had on a maroon Circuit City shirt. I guess he had carried a grudge from high school, and he was a major recruit for Oklahoma State University. In high school, I had scored two touchdowns against him; I was a little better than average.

He said, "I see you work at Circuit City."

I was really embarrassed by this at the time. I thought I should have been doing a little better in life; plus, he put me down. So, instead of getting mad, I just turned it around and said, "It's paying the bills while I'm back in school."

A teachable moment to myself: Don't let people hurt you.

I remember another particular time when I was really down. I went to the counselor, Marleen West. She was the sweetest woman in the world, and her husband is a Pastor.

I sat down in Mrs. West's office, and times were so hard; I said, "Mrs. West, I'm going to quit school."

Her first reaction was that she got up and closed the door. She said, "Baby, I will not let you quit. Do you see what's happening to our black boys? I will help you." She looked in her computer files and saw I only needed 15 credit hours to graduate. She looked at me and said, "Do you know how many men would love to be sitting in your position? There, son. I will be here."

She was telling me how few hours I had left to go because she could see I was burning out fast. She motivated me to stay, and I love Mrs. West for it.

Along the way, I had someone else to take me in and to motivate me—Mrs. Washington from the church. I was in the computer lab, struggling. The instructors would give us assignments to complete. Even though they gave us a book to walk us through it all, I still struggled. Mrs. Washington would come in and make me do the assignments, but she also helped me with them. I was motivated again by perseverance.

My life changed 11,000 percent because I finished getting my degrees. All those places that were denied to me because I didn't have a college degree—now I'm very marketable. Before I graduated college, I wanted to get into pharmaceuticals. I asked around, but they said you need a college degree for that—door-shut-in-face again. I only needed a few semesters to graduate. Not too much time later, I graduated college with a Bachelor of Science in Business Administration after obtaining an Associate's degree in Liberal Arts.

CHAPTER 5

PERSISTENCE PAYS OFF

CHAPTER 5

While maintaining my job at Circuit City, pharmaceutical companies told me I needed to do something sales-related to get started in pharmaceuticals. They advised me to work at Payless Shoes to get some experience.

One day, I met a guy who works for Pfizer. I went to his house and left my resume, which was stellar. He said I called so much that he stopped answering his phone. He was scared I might have been at his house. I figured persistence pays off, though I still had two semesters of college left.

I had been told that this manager, Ken Clemons, was really nice and I needed to look him up. I'm not sure how I found out where he lived, but I got all my award trophies together and headed to his house. Crazy, I know. It sounds bold, but if you really want something, don't let anything stop you.

Anyway, I knocked on the door, and when he opened it, I asked his name to make sure I was at the right place. The name checked out. So I said to him, "My name is Derrick Reynolds, and I'm determined to get into pharmaceuticals."

He had this look on his face like, "I know this guy didn't just show up at my house." He let me in with my box of trophies and awards. The conversation wasn't very long. I told him what I planned to do if he hired me, which was that I would be his top salesman because I've already accomplished greatness. Then I told him I had two semesters to go to graduate college (this was me networking with him), and he said to check back with him when I graduate. Remember, two semesters is a year. So then I told him, okay, and I left. Ken is still one of the top managers in Oklahoma, possibly in the nation, and eventually, he did hire me.

Even when I was down to my last semester, I talked to other pharmaceutical reps, but none of them were helpful.

Thinking outside of the box

I finally told myself that I will give it my best effort to get a job within about six weeks.

I printed up a bunch of resumes and went to doctor's offices, and whenever a rep would come out, I would give them a resume. I met one rep named Phillip, who told me the same thing, "I'll see you when you graduate."

Once I graduated, I got on with Glaxo Smith-Kline Pharmaceuticals and had worked there for two years when I won the President's Club. This is the top salesman in the country. I was really happy then (here we go again). The guy who hired me started turning on me, naturally. If a manager hires you, normally, they will leave you alone—not Derrick. This guy made my life hell, even after winning the top salesman in the country.

The winner is usually in the top 3% of the company. If you win the President's Club, they give you a trip and a cash prize, which is a good perk about being in the pharmaceutical job. After winning the award, I remember this one time there were three of us on a team that was on a conference call with our manager. My sister-in-law was there, and I had my phone on speakerphone. I never felt like an equal on that team. My manager said to Salesman 1, "You better hook a trailer up to carry that big check to the bank!"

Then he said to Salesman 2 (which was his favorite), "The missus is going to have a lot of money to spend on your upcoming trip!"

I'm Salesman 3, and it was my turn to be acknowledged, but he never said anything to me. My sister-in-law was livid. She wanted to say something to him on the conference call because he didn't acknowledge me, but I wouldn't let her. I told her it was like that all the time. I think it was about a month later I asked him if he was prejudiced, but he denied it.

I'd had enough and was preparing to leave. So I asked him why he was a micro-manager, and he said to me, "You can be a poor performer in a high-producing territory."

I challenged him on that by saying, "Remember, I won the top sales award in the country." So he put me on a Performance Improvement Plan (PIP), which isn't a good thing (you must have thick skin). The plan consists of 30, 60, or 90 days of probation. My first 30 days passed. I have four kids and a wife, and this guy is trying to fire me—and I'm the breadwinner of the family.

I asked him if I was off of probation, and he said no, so now I'm on 60 days of probation, and it passed. If you get to the end of 90 days of probation, you're fired. I was really scared; I was trying to find a job because I couldn't afford to get fired. And, for doing nothing wrong.

I found another job, but I was keeping it quiet until everything blew up, so I asked again, "Am I off probation?"

And he smiled and said, "Yes, I just wanted you to sweat a little." What an ASSHOLE. I never did anything wrong in the first place, and people were telling me that was a lawsuit, playing with my emotions like that. But, that's just another reason why I'm so strong today.

I finally left for another job; a Japanese Pharmaceutical Company called Eisai. They really treat you like you're somebody. I stayed there for twelve years, and I won the President's Club four times. The only reason I left was because they laid the entire sales force off. It wasn't long after I got laid off that I landed on my feet again. I started working for Endo Pharmaceuticals in the pain division, which was a whole new world to me.

I was there for two years when they had a major layoff. I got the ax again, but before I left, I won the President's Club again. We won a trip to Spain, but they were having some trouble over there, so they gave us a $10,000 check instead. It's not so bad; getting laid off comes with the job sometimes.

I took a job working for a top pharmacy chain when my boss, Rhonda Demarest, gave me a chance. My title is Regional Account Executive. This company is great to work for, and they take good care of you. I have been with the company for almost four years now. I've won the President's Club twice, and I'm trending to win another, but it's going to be a close race. If I win, that will be three wins in four years, which is not too bad.

I want to say to everyone: **You have heard my story now, and know I went through a lot of not giving up and never letting people's words or actions cause me to do something irrational.**

In your situation, whether it's your job, a bad marriage, your church makes you mad, whatever it is, just stop; then say, "Will this situation change in six months?"

If your answer is no, then change your situation. I have learned people always want to bring you down when you're trying to do something with your life. I say, set some goals because you can't get there without a road map. The most important thing to remember is to make sure you're around positive and successful people.

When I set my goals, I wanted to be around successful and positive people, and I wanted to make a six-figure salary and buy a new vehicle. I wanted to put my kids in a good school, and I wanted to join an investment club. I was one of the people who started our investment club four years ago, and we are finally starting to see the money grow.

Write a book or be a motivational speaker; we all have gifts and talents. We just have to find out what they are.

I've just told you all my goals that I set for myself during the last ten years, and I accomplished all of them. Guess what?

I'M GETTING READY TO SET SOME NEW GOALS!

Have you ever watched the movie *War Room*? One of the lead roles, Ms. Clara, explains a war room is where an army gathers before a war to plan their strategy. She always wrote her prayers down on paper and put them on the wall in her prayer closet, which she called her war room.

Write down your goals and place them in your closet or your bedroom. I did it! Then I was blessed with 20 goals that came true. It works, and you won't know until you try it. Trust me, it worked for me; it will work for you! So try it.

It's your turn! Set 3 goals and follow them until it's time to set some new ones.

1. _____
2. _____
3. _____

YOU'VE GOT THIS! LET'S ROLL!
IT'S YOUR TURN! I BELIEVE IN YOU!
YOU WILL WIN!
DON'T QUIT!

ACKNOWLEDGEMENTS

I'm truly proud of my kids: Katero, Dominique, Derrick II, & De' Marius—The Reynolds Boys!!

I would also like to thank my best friend, Gary Savage, as well as Mr. Joe Clark, Lynell Powell, Ronald Petty, Rev. Potter, Rev. Dawson, Mrs. Sheila Stevenson, Mrs. Ruth Washington, and Mrs. Marleen West for helping me at different times in my life.

And I would also like to acknowledge the special people who were in my life that have passed on: the late Raymond Ratliff Sr, Mr. Jimison Clark, and Gormilla Stovall.

ABOUT THE AUTHOR

Derrick Reynolds is a family man, coach, and motivational speaker, as well as a highly successful, driven college graduate and marketing professional. If you need a coach, or someone who can help motivate you or your team, please reach out via the email address listed below.

Also, if you have a business and you need help increasing your profits, you can email <u>DrSuccess509@gmail.com</u> for guidance and services today.

Printed in the United States
by Baker & Taylor Publisher Services